For Lupina, Rosie, and Kapik, wherever you are...

Ronald J. Lebeck

Tangled Vines -
A *Daggers of Darkness* story

The Art of Tangled Vines

By
Ronald J. Lebeck

Ronald J. Lebeck

Copyright © 2017 by Ronald J. Lebeck

All rights reserved. This book or any portion thereof may not be reproduced or used in any manner whatsoever without the express written permission of the author except for the use of brief quotations in a book review.

Printed in the United States of America

First Printing, 2017

Cover and interior art by Ronald J. Lebeck

ISBN-10: 1978178395
ISBN-13: 978-1978178397

Table of Contents

Preface vii

Acknowledgements ix

Tools of the Trade xi

Craig Nicolini and the Gals 1

Bren-Khy'an – Armored 3

Bren-Khy'an - Unarmored 5

The Blade of Mûr Tua'ansa 7

Ilen-Saa'an – "Deep in Thought" 9

Ilen-Saa'an – Family Portrait 11

Ilen-Saa'an – Color Portrait 13

Ilen-Jaa'an – "Cover Shoot" 15

Ilen-Ada'an – Saa'an's Grandmother 17

Ilen-Saa'an's Speeder Bike 19

Tsel-Ami'an – Color Portrait 21

Tsel-Asa'an – Color Portrait 23

Lady Nemi-Mer'ana – "Tea Time" 25

Lady Pren-Dre'ana – Color Portrait 27

Frer-Sha'an - Healer 29

Captain James Daugherty – Military Portrait 31

Fey Dark Fire's Android Avatar 33

Mûr Zhæn 35

R'Hari – Keori Super Model 37

K'ratori Huntress 39

Ilen-Khy'an Nicolini – "Grown Up" 41

About the Author 43

Preface

Tangled Vines is a side story in my *Daggers of Darkness* series, which begins between book #1, *Into the Black*, and book #2, *The Heart of Élendor*.

I wrote this story to help explain more in depth the people, culture, and traditions of the native inhabitants of Mûr Zhæn, the homeworld of the crew of the exploration vessel, *Chel-Sar Se'nika*, who were rescued in the first story and are a major part of the main story arc. It follows the life of a young human male from Terra by the name of Craig Nicolini, whose parents are part of the first Terran diplomatic mission setting up the new embassy in the capital of the Mûr Tua'ansa Star Empire. Craig makes friends, has some interesting adventures, learns new things, and ultimately finds love on a world that is quite different from any other he has been on.

I was going to add the artwork to the *Tangled Vines* book, but after finding out what the publisher determined the "Minimum Price Threshold" would be, I quickly decided to strip out the art section and create this companion art book to keep the cost of the novel down for my readers—it would have been beyond the ability for most to afford, in my opinion. If you have read the story, I hope you'll like the artwork that goes along with it.

Sincerely,

Ronald J. Lebeck
Author and Artist

Ronald J. Lebeck

Acknowledgements

I wish to thank all of my online readers who have encouraged me to write this story, and also the fine folks who run SoFurry.com who provided a place for my drawings and writings to be displayed and noticed by the fans of anthro art and stories.

Ronald J. Lebeck

Tools of the Trade

Tools of the Trade

For those who may be interested in knowing what I've used to draw my characters, here is a list of items that I usually use:

- 0.5 mm mechanical pencil with HB lead
- 0.1 mm illustrator's pen with black India ink
- graphite sticks, 6B and 2H
- Prismacolor colored pencils
- various blending and shading tools, such as blending stumps and folded paper towels
- white vinyl "click" eraser
- 6" aircraft grade stainless steel engineer's rule
- architect's three-edge scale

The paper that I usually draw my originals on is Georgia-Pacific's "Everyday Copy & Print", 92 brightness, 8.5"x11". After the drawing is finished, I usually scan at 300 dpi, 48-bit color (for the color drawings) or 16-bit grayscale (for the black and white drawing). Text is added on the computer after scanning.

Ronald J. Lebeck

Craig Nicolini and the Gals

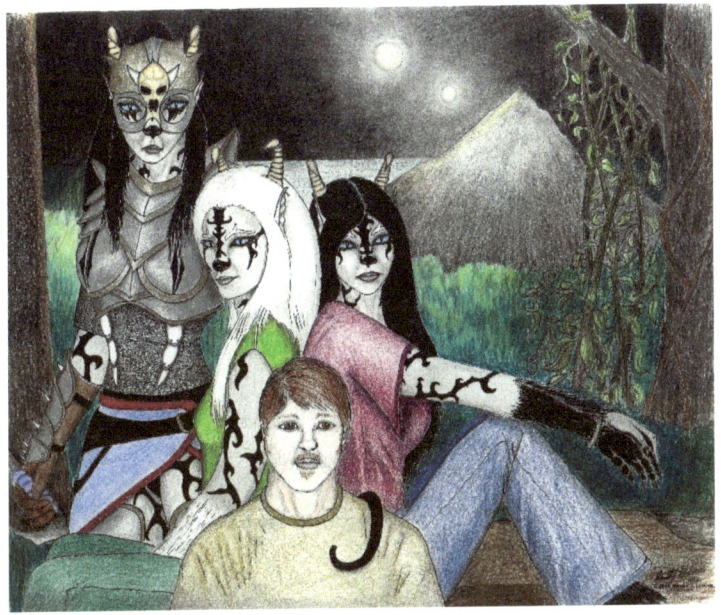

I used this as the cover art for the print book and the e-book. From left to right: Bren-Khy'an, Tsel-Ami'an, Craig Nicolini, and Ilen-Saa'an. In the background is the valley of *Aja-we'nes* mentioned in chapter 9, and the twin moons, .

Ronald J. Lebeck

Bren-Khy'an – Armored

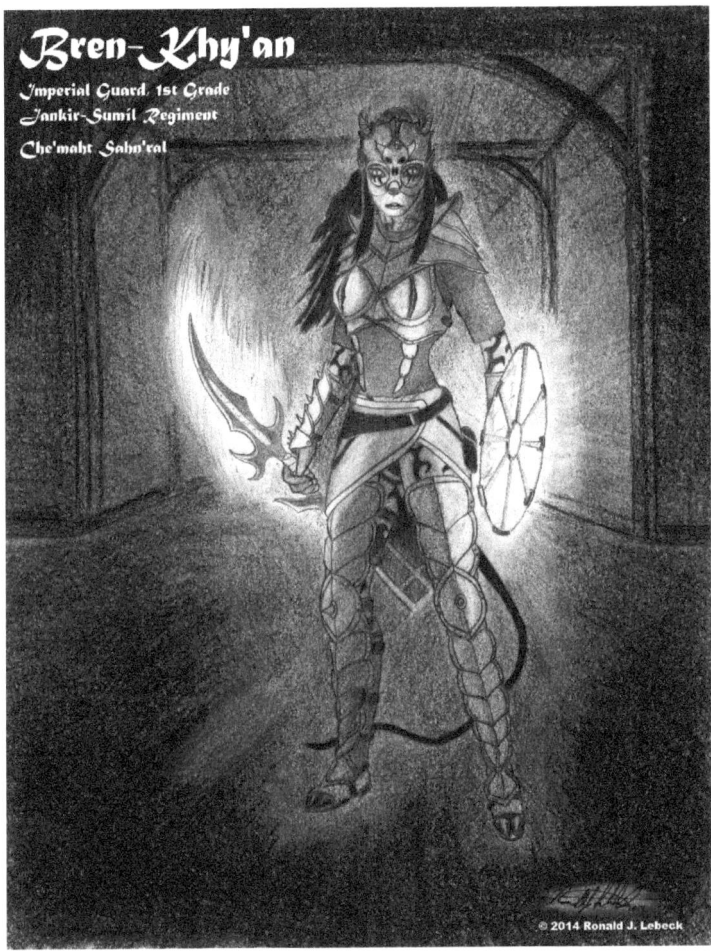

Bren-Khy'an, Imperial Guard 1st Grade in the Jankir-Sumíl Regiment of the Che'maht Sahn'rah (the elite personal guard of Empress Krel-Mri'ana).

Bren-Khy'an is 7 ft. 10 in. tall, and an imposing, definitely no-nonsense, warrior whose loyalty to the Empress is absolute. She has an "energy shield" on her left arm (upon a certain movement, the eight telescoping arms shoot out and a force-field engages from the emitters at the ends). In her right hand is a fully functional "Blade of Mûr Tua'ansa" - it is currently in the "energized" state, with the forward part emitting disruptor energies, ready to cause death and destruction to anything it touches. The weapon is specially "tuned" to its "owner", so that in the hands of anyone else, it would just be a sharp blade (she can actually use it as such, if need be, though).

Bren-Khy'an – Unarmored

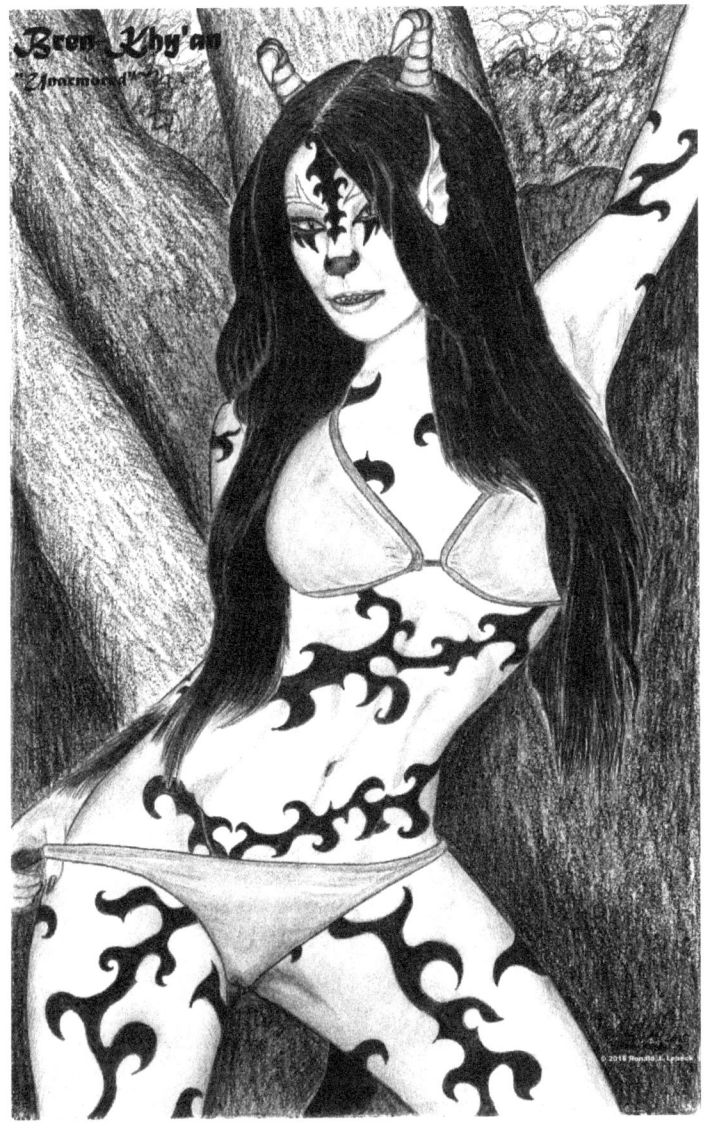

After a little (okay, a *lot*) of persuading, I've convinced Bren-Khy'an to do a "cheesecake" pose in a bikini. It isn't often (read as "freakin' rare") that a member of the elite

Ronald J. Lebeck

Imperial Guard unit that protects the Empress ever let it be known that they *do* have a "softer" side (usually, even their own families are terrified of them), so take a good look as you probably won't see one posing like this again in a Terran lifetime. I'm gonna *owe* her big time for this, no doubt. :^O

"What's that Khy'an? Well, you *ARE* a sexy babe, so wah! Just because you're gonna have a lot of guys wanting your comm address, doesn't mean...ERK! (*gasps for air*) Put...me...down...*please*! I-I'll rub your...ankles..." (*thump!*) (Thinks to self: "*The things I do for art...sheesh!*")

The Blade of Mûr Tua'ansa

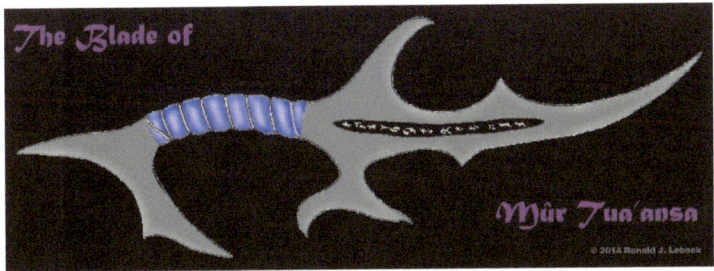

This is -- I guess you could say -- the "national weapon" of the Mûr Tua'ansa people. I have it depicted in the art of their world, though here is a close up. I drew it by hand, and then colored it in Photoshop.

Ronald J. Lebeck

Ilen-Saa'an – "Deep in Thought"

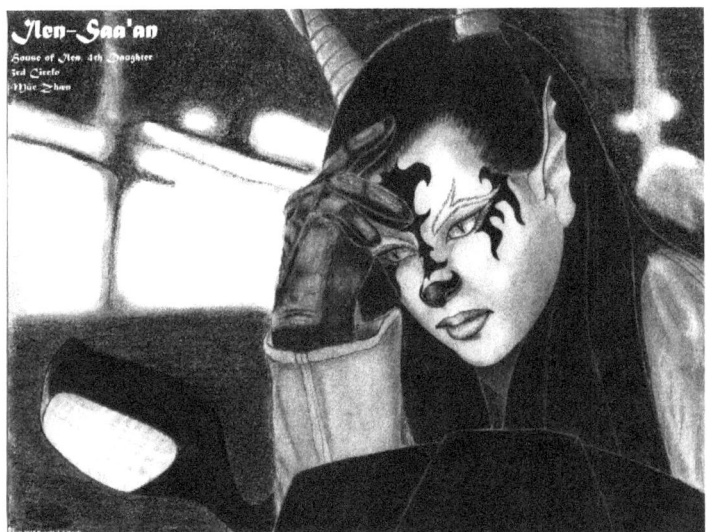

Here is Ilen-Saa'an, of the House of Ilen, where she is 4th Daughter in a 3rd Circle house (think "lower class"). She is thinking about how much of a mess her life has just become because of a bumbling son of human diplomats assigned to her world. Eventually, Ilen-Saa'an can't stop thinking of the human guy (hence this drawing), and feels that her life has suddenly been turned upside-down.

Ronald J. Lebeck

Ilen-Saa'an – Family Portrait

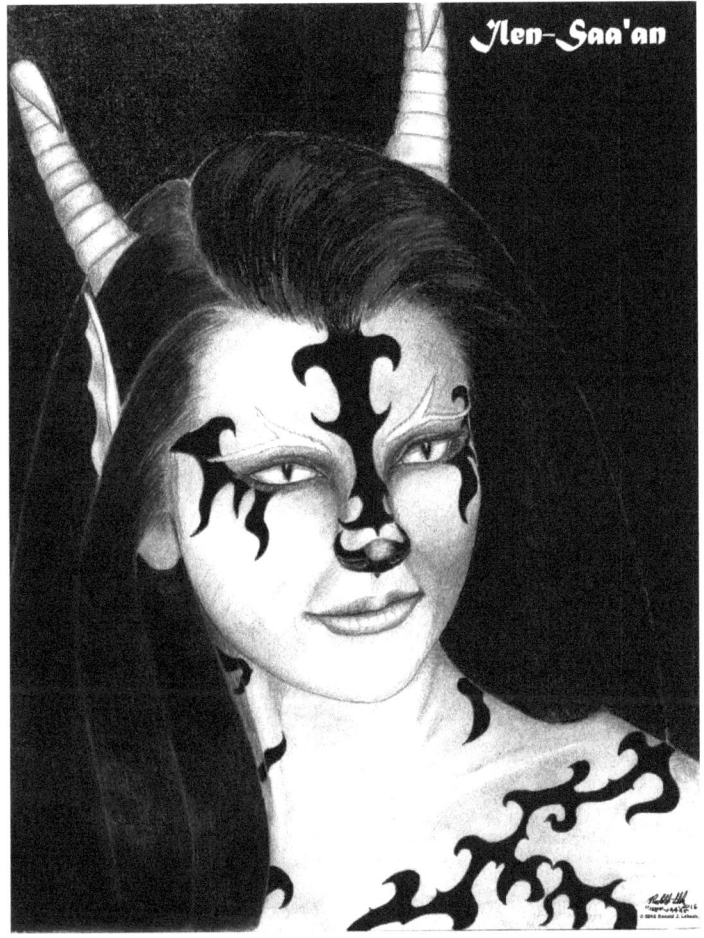

Here's a portrait of Ilen-Saa'an (like one that the family would have hanging on a wall). I tried to make her look like the first drawing, though with a different (more formal?) hairstyle.

Ronald J. Lebeck

Ilen-Saa'an – Color Portrait

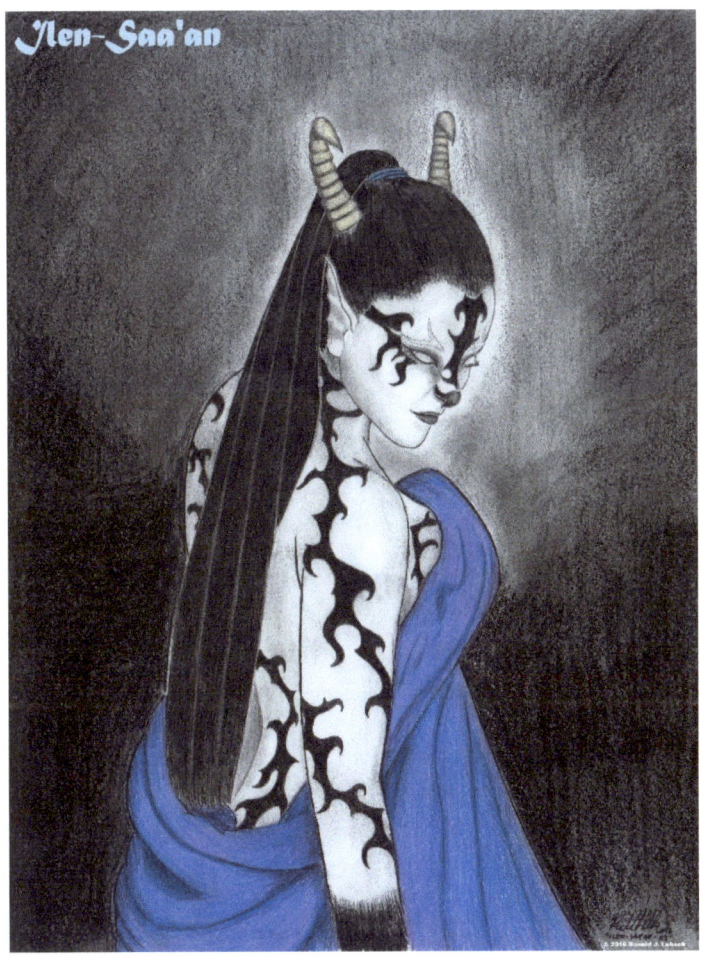

Here is another view of Ilen-Saa'an.

Ronald J. Lebeck

Ilen-Jaa'an – "Cover Shoot"

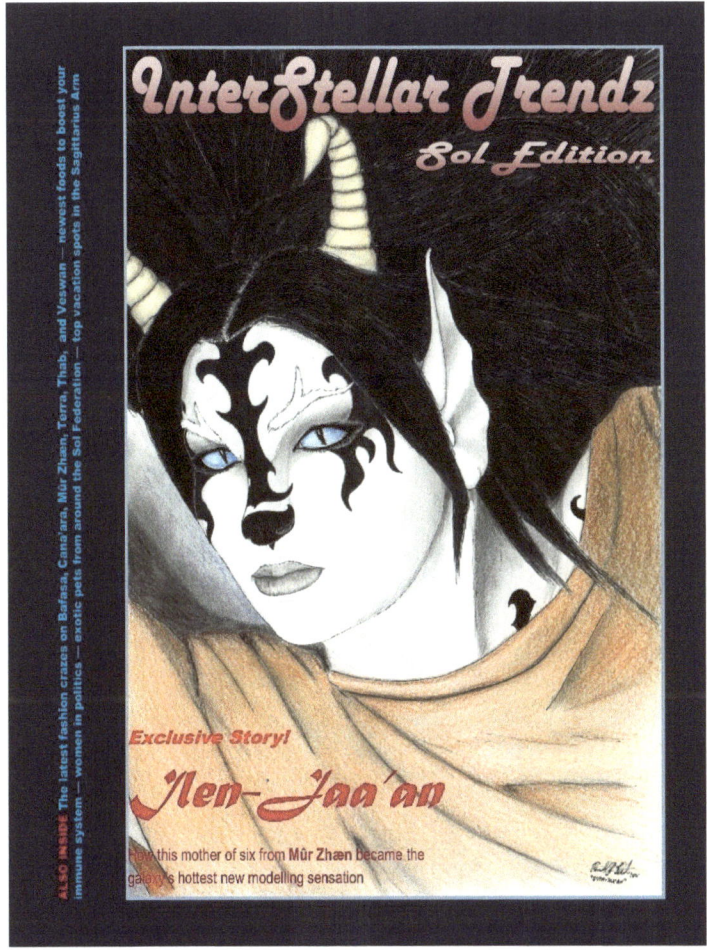

Here's Ilen-Jaa'an, Ilen-Saa'an's mother. At some point in the story, Craig sends a "family photo" of Ilen-Saa'an's family back to friends of his on Terra. Eventually, a modelling agency "discovers" her, and offers Ilen-Jaa'an a lucrative contract, which will eventually raise the status of House Ilen back on Mûr Zhæn.

Ronald J. Lebeck

Ilen-Ada'an – Saa'an's Grandmother

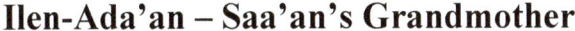

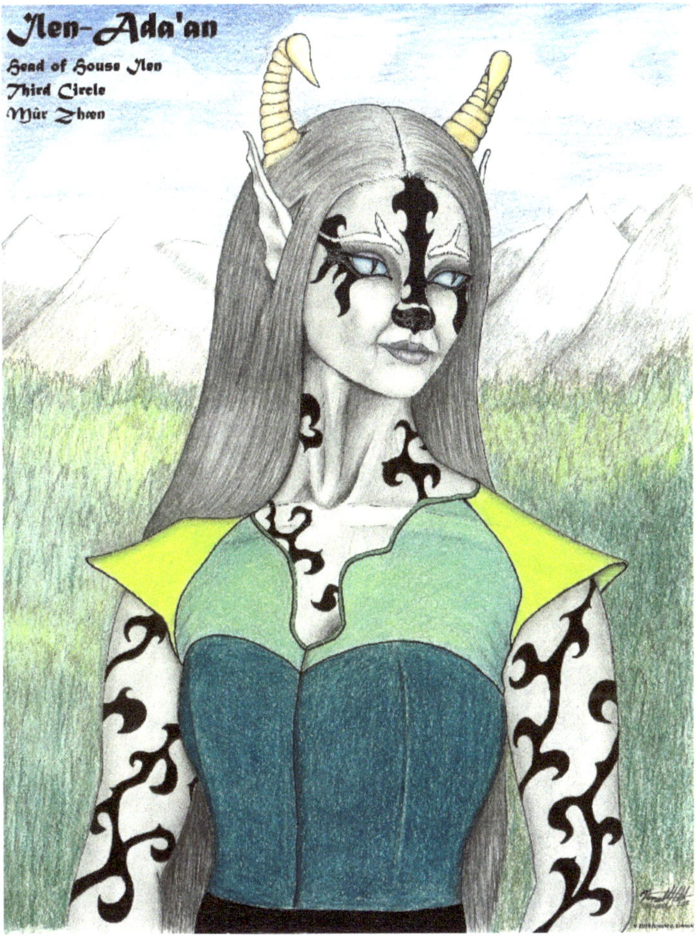

Here's Ilen-Ada'an, the current head of House Ilen, the mother of Ilen-Jaa'an, and the grandmother of Ilen-Saa'an. Ilen-Ada'an is 161 Mûr Zhæn years old (that puts her a 850 Std. Terran Years of age -- it was the year 1663 here on our world when she was born!), and she's currently 9 ft. tall with approximately another 30-40 Mûr Zhæn years left ahead of her.

Ronald J. Lebeck

Ilen-Saa'an's Speeder Bike

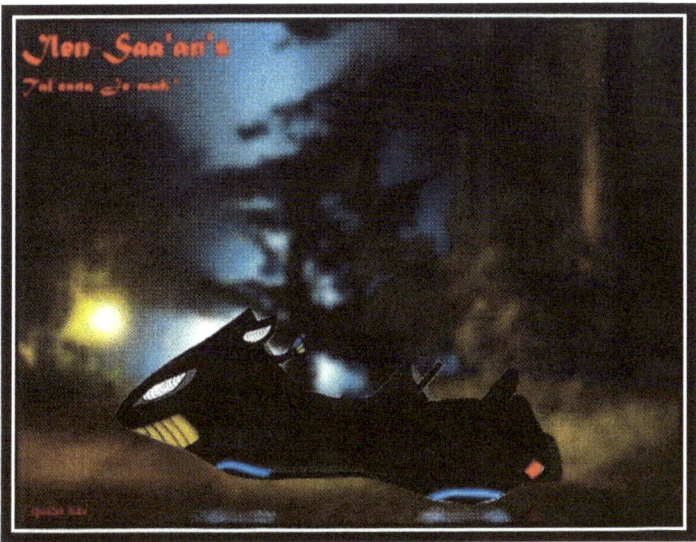

Here's Ilen-Saa'an's *Tal'esna Je-mah*, a particular two-seater model of speeder bike. The bike has three anti-grav repulsor units plus a thruster for lift and propulsion. It is capable of achieving a top speed of 200 km/hr and an altitude of 1.0 km AGL (Above Ground Level), with a range of approximately 14 days of use before recharging (energy storage cells, fuel, etc.). The nose of the bike contains an air intake for cooling, a mini deflector array (for avoiding being hit by flying creatures, branches or small objects), and sensors. The driver has a view screen that displays pertinent performance data, enhanced visual (forward and rear views), and navigational data. The handlebars curve inward (unlike our current motorcycles); the front set has thumb controls on each side that control various bike functions. The top portion of the two rear anti-grav units contain storage compartments for items. The legs of the driver and passenger are provided further protection by molded in side fairings. Ilen-Saa'an has opted for the entertainment system (a comm system and security system are standard). On the underside (not shown in this view) is a three-point retractable stand for the bike to rest on when the anti-grav units are switched off to save power.

    I drew the basic outline of the bike on Georgia-Pacific's "Everyday Copy & Print" paper using a 0.5 mm mechanical pencil with HB lead, inked it with a Pilot G-2 05 pen with black gel ink, and then used the Pixlr online editor (https://www.pixlr.com/editor) to add first the background (a freely available stock photo), which I added a blur to put the focus on the bike, and then added the bike as a 2nd layer. Coloring, shading, and touch-ups were all done using Pixlr. Text was added in Windows Paint.

Tsel-Ami'an – Color Portrait

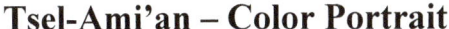

    Here's Tsel-Ami'an, the best friend and confidant of Ilen-Saa'an. She's one of the Khea Mûr Tua'ansa. In addition to the abilities of telepathy, telekinesis, and teleportation, Ami'an—being one of the Khea—always knows instinctually where the sacred spring known as *Mûr thel-Raleen* is located. Ami'an also has one other very unique skill, that of foreknowledge.

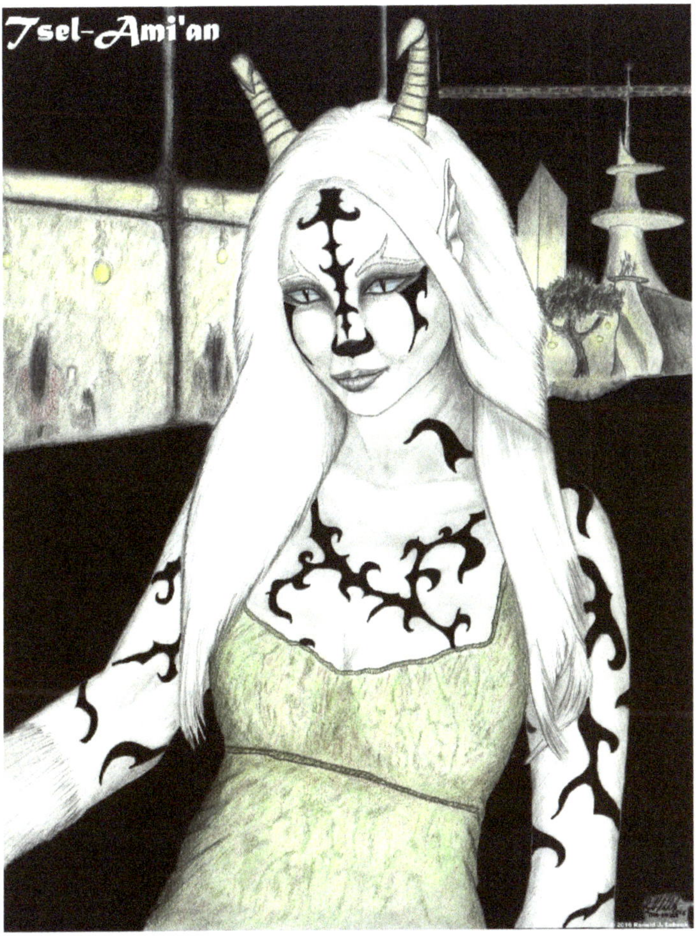

Ronald J. Lebeck

Tsel-Asa'an – Color Portrait

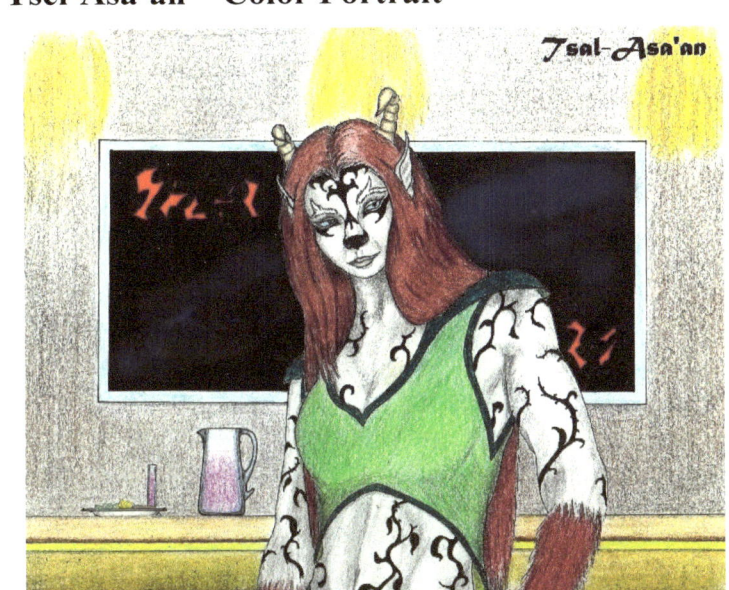

Here's a drawing of Tsal-Asa'an, the cousin of Tsel-Ami'an's mother, and the owner of "*The Drift*". Although she is a Khea, Tsal-Asa'an has an odd genetic mutation that gave her red hair instead of the usual white. Tsal-Asa'an is not a small woman, and her size can be rather intimidating. Usually rather outgoing and jovial, Tsal-Asa'an is something of a flirt and she enjoys hitting on Craig, much to the Ilen-Saa'an's annoyance.

Ronald J. Lebeck

Lady Nemi-Mer'ana – "Tea Time"

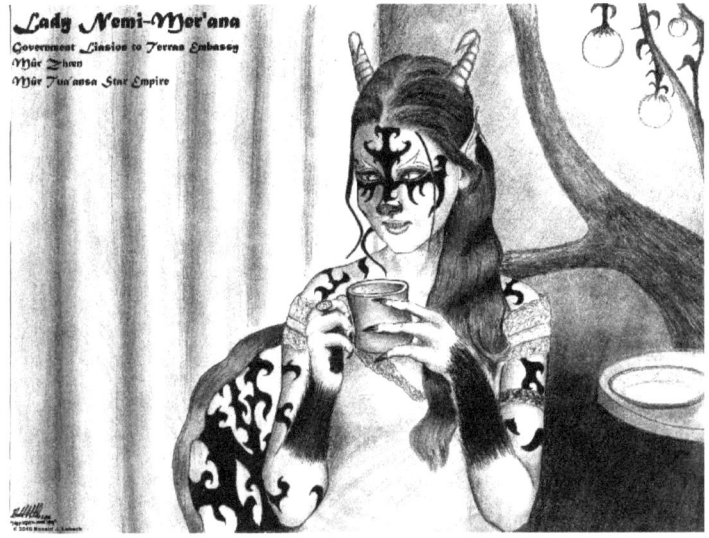

Here's Lady Nemi-Mer'ana, of the Diplomatic Circle, Mûr Tua'ansa Star Empire. She is the official government liaison to the Terran Embassy, located on Mûr Zhæn in the capital city of Zhæn'ana. Given her position, she is in regular contact with the ambassadorial staff of the Terran Embassy, and frequently visits William and Cassandra Nicolini, who are the human diplomatic officials in charge of Cultural Exchange. For an otherwise typical Mûr Tua'ansa woman, Lady Nemi-Mer'ana is a bit on the petite side. However, she is a highly intelligent, quick-witted, strong-willed, calculating diplomat who knows when to be charming and when to "go for the throat", so-to-speak.

Ronald J. Lebeck

Lady Pren-Dre'ana – Color Portrait

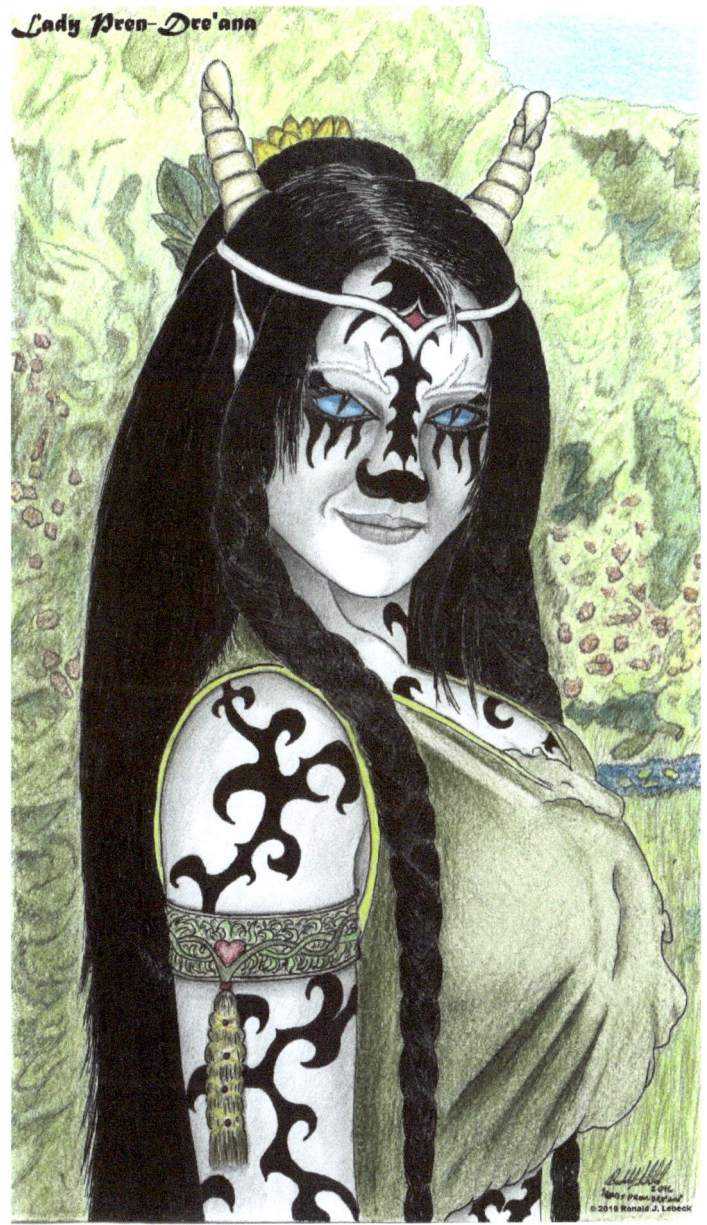

Here's Lady Pren-Dre'ana, the Head Mistress of the Mûr Tua'ansa Star Empire's Diplomatic Circle (she's their equivalent of a Secretary of State, so a very high-level government official). The tassel that you see on her arm bracelet indicates her position as being the head person of what she does (she has another on her other arm, also with one tassel -- there are always two). Lady Pren-Dre'ana has some of her hair tied up in back and there is a flower with some leaves stuck into it. The circlet on her head is silver, and shows that she is higher nobility. Height-wise, she's 8 ft 2 in tall, not sure about her weight, and she's a lot older than one might expect...and currently single. ;)

Frer-Sha'an – Healer

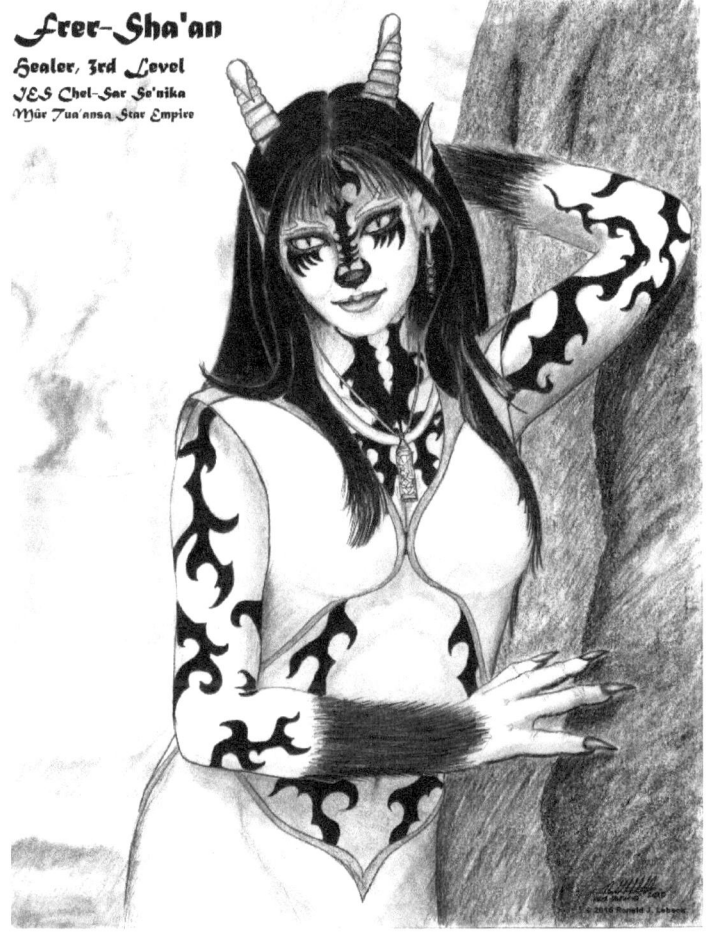

Here's Frer-Sha'an, the healer onboard the I.E.S. *Chel-Sar Se'nika*. She's 7 ft 7 in tall (231.14 cm), 225 lbs (102.06 kg), and 152 Std. Terran years old. Frer-Sha'an has the usual abilities of her people, plus the ability to heal at the Third Level of ability (can regenerate lost limbs and damaged organs), and can create a shield of protective energy about herself and anyone she is trying to protect. Frer-Sha'an has the typical appearance of her people,

Ronald J. Lebeck

though her eyes are a somewhat darker shade of blue (typ. is ice blue, so hers would be a light blue).

Captain James Daugherty – Military Portrait

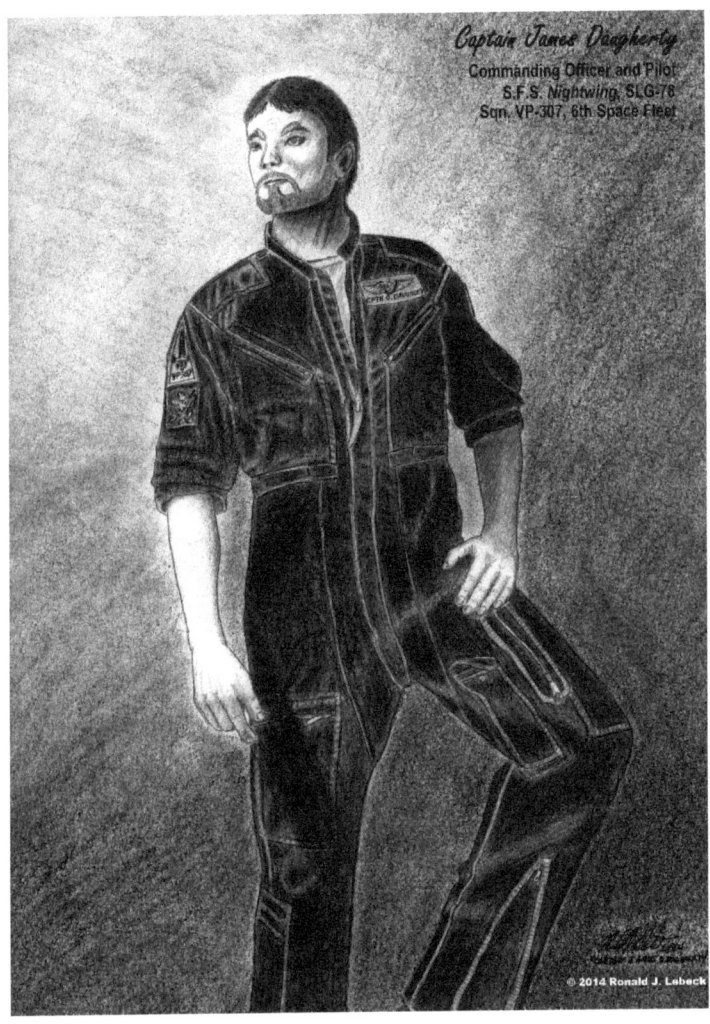

Here's Captain James Daugherty, the commanding officer and pilot of S.F.S. *Nightwing*, SLG-78, attached to squadron VP-307, 6th Space Fleet. James is the twentieth great grandson of MCPO Ron Daugherty (USN, Ret.) and Lupina Daugherty, via their son Cormac, of the original "*Family Tails*" story, which takes place five hundred years earlier. James is a 6 ft 4 in tall "near human" -- he looks mostly human, though he has wolf G.E.L.F. in his ancestry, as can be seen in his lupine eyes, eyebrows, and slightly pointed ears. He has a couple of other traits, such as greatly increased sense of smell, hearing, and stamina, and teeth that are more wolf-like than human. He is shown here in his "combat flight suit", which is different from the usual flight suit-style coveralls that is the usual "uniform of the day" for his crew.

Fey Dark Fire's Android Avatar

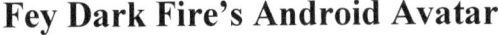

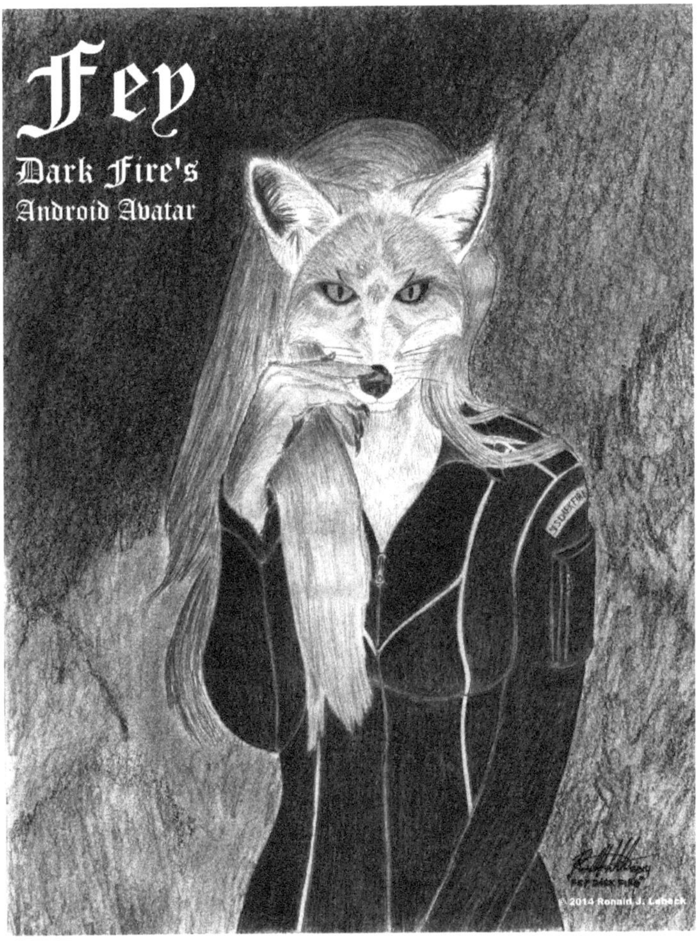

Fey is the ship's A.I. entity who inhabits the computer core onboard the S.F.S. *Dark Fire*, SLG-76, and this is her android avatar. Fey and her crew provided escort to Mûr Zhæn and temporary security at the new Terran Embassy. Fey's android avatar is that of a fox with dark red fur.

Ronald J. Lebeck

Mûr Zhæn

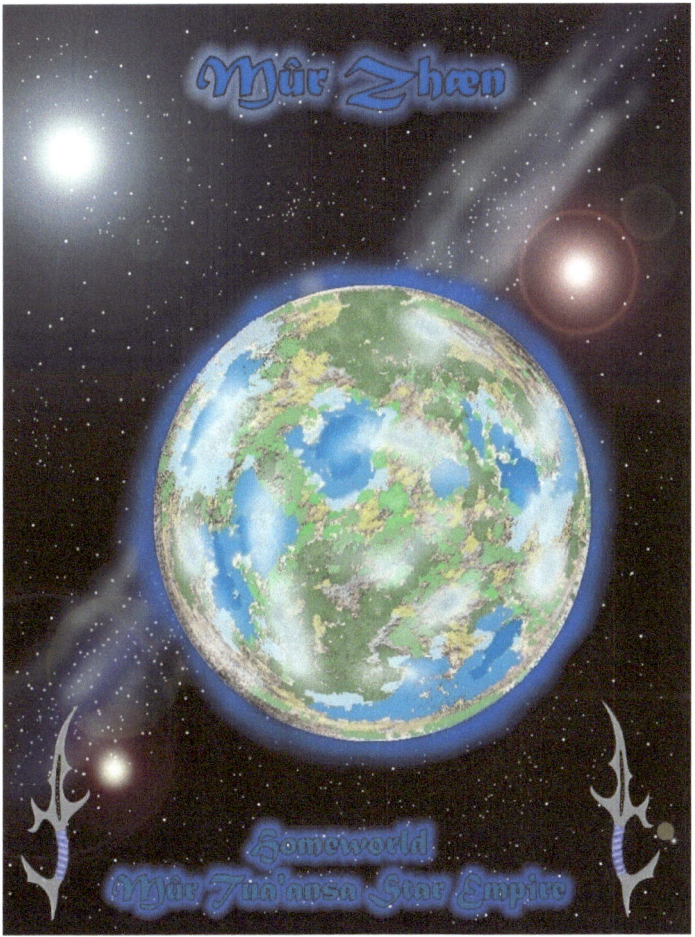

This is the homeworld of Ilen-Saa'an in full color. I generated the world using Fractal Terrains 3, colored it and did nearly everything else in Adobe Photoshop (the blades I drew by hand, scanned, colored, and then added to this picture).

Ronald J. Lebeck

The Art of Tangled Vines

R'Hari – Keori Super Model

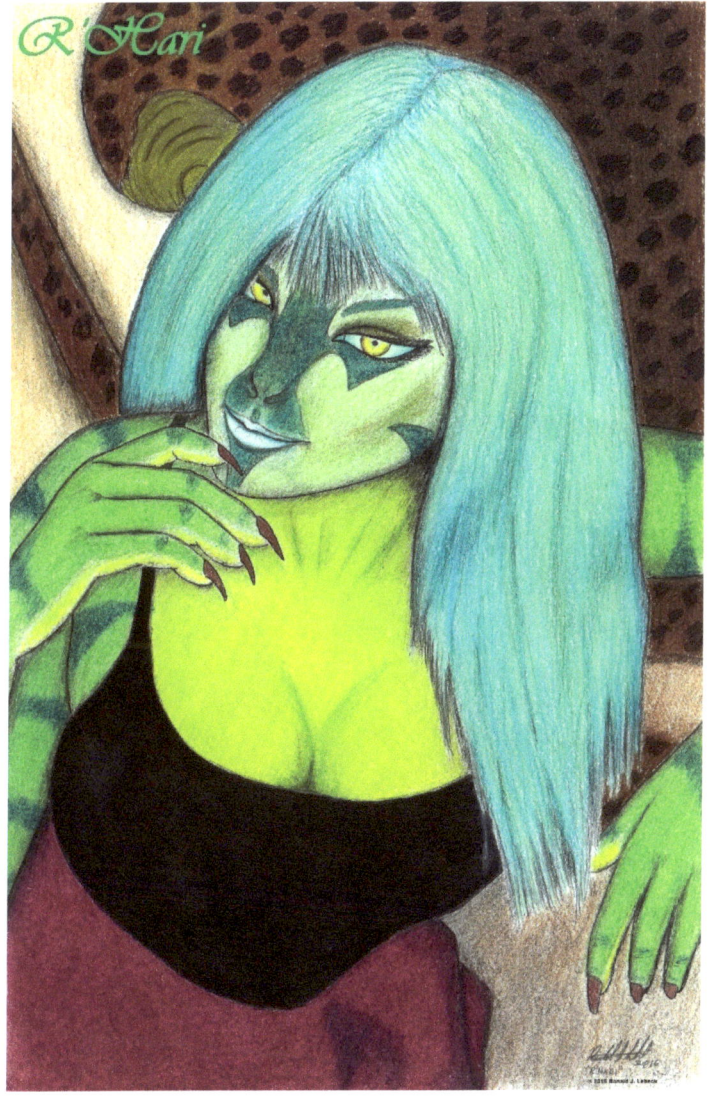

    R'Hari is about 6 ft 5 in tall, she is a Keori, who are by strange circumstance, related to the Élendorians even though their two species evolved on planets in different star systems. This was found to be due to both worlds having been "guided" by the First Ones who "seeded" those worlds after they formed. R'Hari is a top supermodel among the various alien worlds in the Sol Federation of Planets. Like the Élendorians, the Keori are saurian (lizard) with mammalian traits, meaning they're warm-blooded, have smooth skin, they have "hair" of sorts on their heads (it's not quite like what you would think of being hair) that has an iridescent quality similar to some feathers, their young are "live-born" (vs being hatched from an egg), they have tails, and their hands have four fingers and a thumb while their feet have four toes. Keori tend to like heavily forested temperate climates. Keori are strong empaths, though they have no known telepathic ability.

    R'Hari is quite sensual when she walks, and like all of the females of her race, she naturally gives off an exotic spicy musk-like scent.

K'ratori Huntress

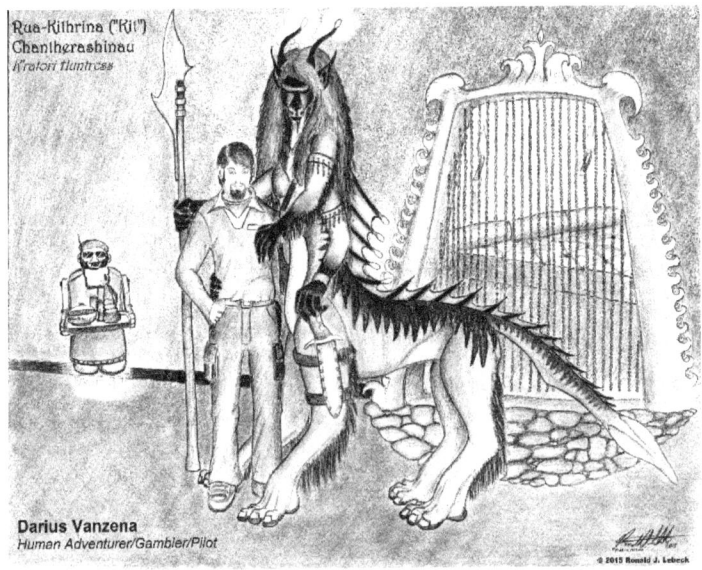

This is Rua-Kithrina ("Kit") Chantherashinau (pronounced: ROO-ah_ki-THRINA chan-THERA-shin-AH-oo), a K'ratori Huntress, and her human male friend, Darius Vanzena.

The K'ratori are a fiercely independent race of quadrupeds, known to never allow themselves to be taken captive if at all possible. They will fight to the death, not willing to give up a "hunt" once they are on one -- due to their cunning, skill with weapons, bravery, and powerful wills, they rarely lose a fight.

The K'ratori are a member of the Sol Federation of Worlds, though mostly for trade and mutual defense.

In appearance, the K'ratori have four legs and a horizontal lower torso, and an upright upper torso with four arms. The head of a K'ratori sports a thick, very coarse, almost cord-like hair that tends towards a smoky reddish color. There are two large pointed, upswept ears, two black colored "stalks" on top of the head ending in a bioluminescent "bulb" -- these can move independently of each other. The face is similar in some ways to an aquatic Terran animal known as a sea horse, though with a shorter muzzle. The one odd feature is the single horizontal eye slit, that -- if one could look closely -- seems to have a faint inner glow, either a dull reddish or a deep bluish. This is due to the unusual abilities of "infravision" (the ability to see deep into the infrared portion of the light spectrum) and "ultravision" (the ability to see deep into the ultraviolet portion of the light spectrum). A K'ratori may use either at will as conditions require. A K'ratori's skin is smooth for the most part, can be of various colors, though blends into black on the forearms and hands. The back of all K'Ratori have a dark stripe-like pattern. The back edge of a K'ratori's legs have "feathering" the same color and texture as on the head. The majority of a K'ratori's face and muzzle are black fading to lighter smoky-colored area along the sides of their muzzle. Also on the back of both the upper and lower torso are black spines -- the upper five end in a bioluminescent "bulb", while the rest end in extremely sharp, poisonous points. The barbs can be raised or lowered depending on the mood of a K'ratori. The "bulbs" can change color and intensity upon mood and/or need.

Despite their size, K'ratori are naturally stealthy, able to move silently and slowly. K'ratori can also run quickly, typically by lowering their upper torso (leaning forward) -- the faster they are running, the lower their upper torso will likely be. Their sense of smell and hearing is such that they similar to a a Terran wolf in ability.

"Kit" and her friend Darius have sort of a business partnership, and have been friends for several years. They have shared many interesting adventures, and it's rumored that they may also have a "friends with benefits" type of relationship. Personality-wise, they are quite opposite from one another in many ways -- Darius tends to be a risk-taker and a gambler, and more of a spur-of-the-moment person; Kit, while brave, is not foolhardy, and she tends to be the more serious of the two...also the more aggressive. Kit does have a wicked sense of humor, carefully plans her hunts, and can be extremely single-minded at times.

In this scene, Kit and Darius are posing together, which shows the size comparison between the two (Darius is approximately 5" 11" tall, and weighs about 190 lbs.). In the background and to the viewer's left is a servebot that Darius won in a card game.

Ronald J. Lebeck

Ilen-Khy'an Nicolini – "Grown Up"

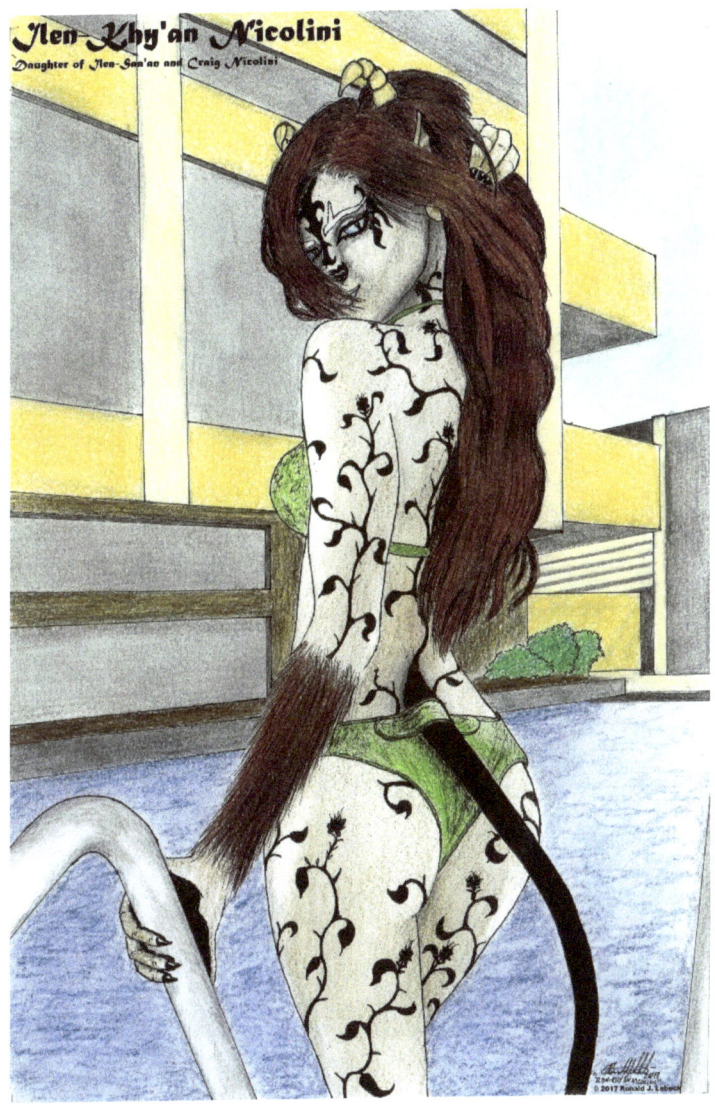

Here's Ilen-Khy'an Nicolini, the daughter of Ilen-Saa'an and Craig Nicolini. Craig and Saa'an end up having a daughter, though not by normal means. Biologically, the two would be incapable of having a child together...however, they sought out a geneticist on Mûr Zhæn by the name of Aama-Ael'an to see if she would be able to give them a definitive answer as to whether or not intervention would be possible to create a viable offspring. Little did they know at the time, the geneticist, Aama-Ael'an, was actually a First One by the name of A'amahi Afer-ael'ena, one of shape-changing Nomenara, who had been patiently waiting over seven billion years for the two to come together. A'amahi Afer-ael'ena was able to manipulate the genetic material donated by Saa'an and Craig so that Saa'an could become pregnant.

    Ilen-Khy'an Nicolini eventually was born quite healthy, and would eventually have children of her own. She is literally a product of two worlds, with the best features and abilities of both her Mûr Tua'ansa mother and her human father. She has her mother's clan name, and her given name is that of her godmother, Bren-Khy'an.

    So, here she is, all grown up, at the pool of the apartment complex in the Chicago suburbs where Craig's home on Terra is located.

About the Author

Born in Iowa City, Iowa, Ronald J. Lebeck was raised in Burlington, Iowa, Lomax, Illinois and also in Moberly, Missouri, where he graduated from high school. He served his country honorably in the U.S. Navy and later graduated from college.

Other published stories:

Novels:

Family Tails – The Story of a Mixed Family in the Genetic Age
CreateSpace eStore: https://www.createspace.com/5184244

Tangled Vines
CreateSpace eStore: https://www.createspace.com/ 7679280

Short Stories:

The Changed One
CreateSpace eStore: https://www.createspace.com/5341143

The Little Mouse and the Old Wolf
CreateSpace eStore: https://www.createspace.com/7176945

Follow the author on Facebook!

Follow the author on SoFurry!
https://ancientwolf.sofurry.com

Ronald J. Lebeck

www.ingramcontent.com/pod-product-compliance
Lightning Source LLC
Chambersburg PA
CBHW040326220526
45473CB00009B/2583